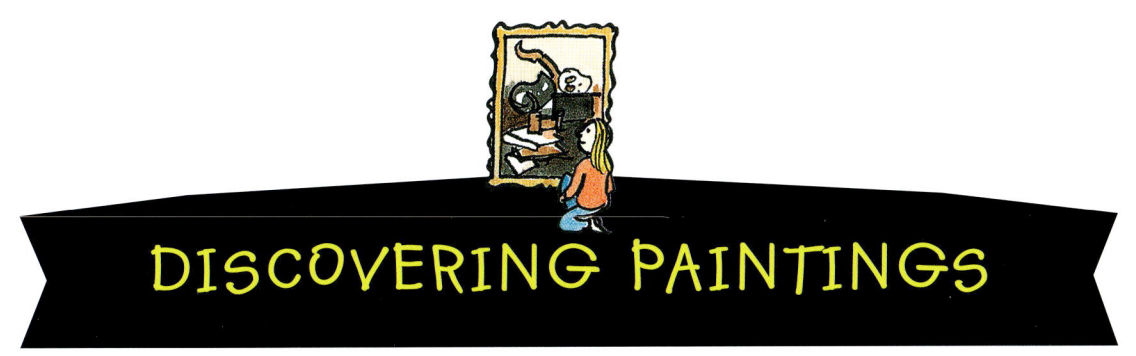

DISCOVERING PAINTINGS

GRISLY & GRUESOME

Ruth Thomson

Chrysalis Education
in association with The National Gallery, London

US publication copyright © 2003 Chrysalis Education

International copyright reserved in all countries.
No part of this book may be reproduced in any form
without written permission from the publisher.

Distributed in the United States by
Smart Apple Media,
1980 Lookout Drive
North Mankato, Minnesota 56003

Copyright © Chrysalis Books PLC 2003
Text © Anne Civardi & Ruth Thomson 2003
Illustrations © National Gallery Company Limited 2003
From an original idea created by National Gallery Company, 2001,
which was generously supported by Mr. and Mrs. Anthony Speelman

ISBN 1 93198 370 4

The Library of Congress control number 2003102565

Editorial manager: Joyce Bentley
Consultant: Erika Langmuir
Educational consultant: Hector Doyle
Design: Mei Lim
Illustrator: Georgie Birkett
Project manager for National Gallery Company: Jan Green

Printed in China

Contents

- 4   About this book
- 5   Using this book
- 6   **Saint Michael triumphant over the Devil with the Donor Antonio Juan** (Bartolomé Bermejo)
- 8   Saint Michael and the Devil
- 9   Saint Michael (Carlo Crivelli)
  Saint Michael (Piero della Francesca)
- 10   **The Death of Actaeon** (Titian)
- 12   Diana and Actaeon
- 13   A Huntsman cutting up a Dead Deer, with Two Deerhounds (Jan Baptist Weenix)
- 14   **Judith in the Tent of Holofernes** (Johann Liss)
- 16   Judith, the Heroine
- 17   Judith (Eglon Hendrick van der Neer)
- 18   **Vanitas Still Life** (Jan Jansz. Treck)
- 20   Vanitas Paintings
- 21   Still Life: An Allegory of the Vanities of Human Life (Harmen Steenwyck)
- 22   **Perseus turning Phineas and his Followers to Stone** (Luca Giordano)
- 24   The Story of Perseus and Andromeda
- 25   Perseus and Andromeda (after Guido Reni)
- 26   **The Execution of Lady Jane Grey** (Paul Delaroche)
- 28   The Story of Lady Jane Grey
- 29   The Beheading of John the Baptist (Pierre-Cécile Puvis de Chavannes)
- 30   Things to do
- 32   Glossary and Index

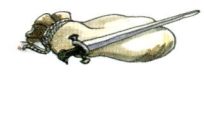

About this book

The pictures in this book have been chosen because each one is part of a thrilling, and often quite gruesome, story—whether a religious story from the Bible, a mythological tale from ancient Greece, or a true historical event.

The picture of *Saint Michael triumphant over the Devil*, for example, is part of a story from the Bible about the struggle between good and evil. This powerful image was painted at a time when most people could not read. Hanging in a church, it would have reminded worshipers of the key moment in this story.

The painting of *Perseus turning Phineas and his Followers to Stone* shows a particularly dramatic moment in the long saga of the daring exploits of Perseus, a mythological ancient Greek hero. At the time when this was painted, Greek myths were well-known and the educated people who saw this picture would have recognized all the main characters in it.

By contrast, *The Execution of Lady Jane Grey* is based on a true event, although the picture was painted almost three hundred years after this took place. As you will soon discover, the artist did not paint the event very accurately. He was far more interested in creating a very dramatic picture.

Ways of telling a story

Although paintings like these can show only frozen moments in a story, artists use all sorts of techniques to help you work out what might have happened before and what might happen next. The most important people in a story are often placed in the center or in the foreground of the painting, and may be more brilliantly lit than everyone else. Their facial expressions, poses, positions, or gestures may tell you how they are feeling and suggest what they have just done or are about to do. Look for these clues as you explore each picture.

Using this book

This book focuses on six grisly and gruesome paintings. There are four sections about each picture that will help you to find out more about it.

 asks questions about the painting, which can all be answered by looking at certain details.

 suggests activities that involve your senses and your imagination.

 gives background information about the painting and includes answers to some of the *Look Closer* questions.

 provides another painting on a similar theme for you to compare and contrast with the first one.

Saint Michael triumphant over the Devil with the Donor Antonio Juan

(ABOUT 1468)
Bartolomé Bermejo

This picture shows part of a story from the Bible, which describes how war broke out in Heaven. Saint Michael, captain of God's army of angels, fought the rebel angels led by the Devil. Saint Michael pushed the Devil out of Heaven and trampled him underfoot, so that he would stay down on earth.

LOOK CLOSER

What is Saint Michael about to do?
How would you describe his expression?

What clue shows that Saint Michael is an angel?
What clues show that he is a soldier?

What can you see reflected in his breastplate?
Where do you think this might be?

The Devil has been made up from three different kinds of animals.
What are they? How many faces does he have?
What is coming out of his belly?

The donor, the person who paid for the picture to be painted,
is the man kneeling on the left.
What clues show you that he was a knight?
Why do you think he is kneeling?

TAKE ACTION

Bermejo has painted Saint Michael with a pearl crown on his head. Find six other places where you can also see pearls.
What other kinds of jewels can you see in the picture?

Where can you find these flowers in the picture?
• poppy
• thistle

The background of the picture is covered in thin leaves of real gold, punched into patterns.
Why do you think the artist did this?
(Clue: think about where the picture might have hung and how it was lit.)

What has the Devil seen that makes him look so scared?

If you were the Devil, how would you persuade Saint Michael not to kill you?

7

READ ABOUT

Saint Michael and the Devil

Saint Michael was seen by both Jews and Christians as their protector against evil. He is one of the most powerful angels, known as archangels. He is usually painted as a soldier, wearing particularly rich armor. In Bermejo's picture, his shiny breastplate reflects the imaginary towers and spires of the city of Heaven.

Saint Michael also carries a sword and shield. He holds the sword ready to cut off the Devil's head and points his crystal shield down towards him. The Devil is shying away in terror at the reflection of his own horrible face.

Antonio Juan, the donor of the picture, was a knight and lord of Tous, a small town in Spain. He paid for this picture to be painted as the center of the altarpiece in his local church. He is shown here reading Psalms from his prayerbook. Bermejo was the greatest 15th-century Spanish painter. He signed his nickname in Latin, on the piece of parchment in front of the donor, as bartolomeus rubeus. "Rubeus" means red, so the artist was probably red-haired.

LOOK FURTHER

(left) Saint Michael (ABOUT 1476)
Carlo Crivelli

(right) Saint Michael (COMPLETED 1469)
Piero della Francesca

Compare how these other artists have painted Saint Michael and the Devil.

Which Saint Michael looks braver? Which shows the more gruesome Devil?

The Death of Actaeon

(ABOUT 1565) **Titian**

S tep into these woods to see the magical thing that has happened. Diana, goddess of the moon and hunting, has punished Actaeon, because while hunting, he saw her bathing naked in a stream.

LOOK CLOSER

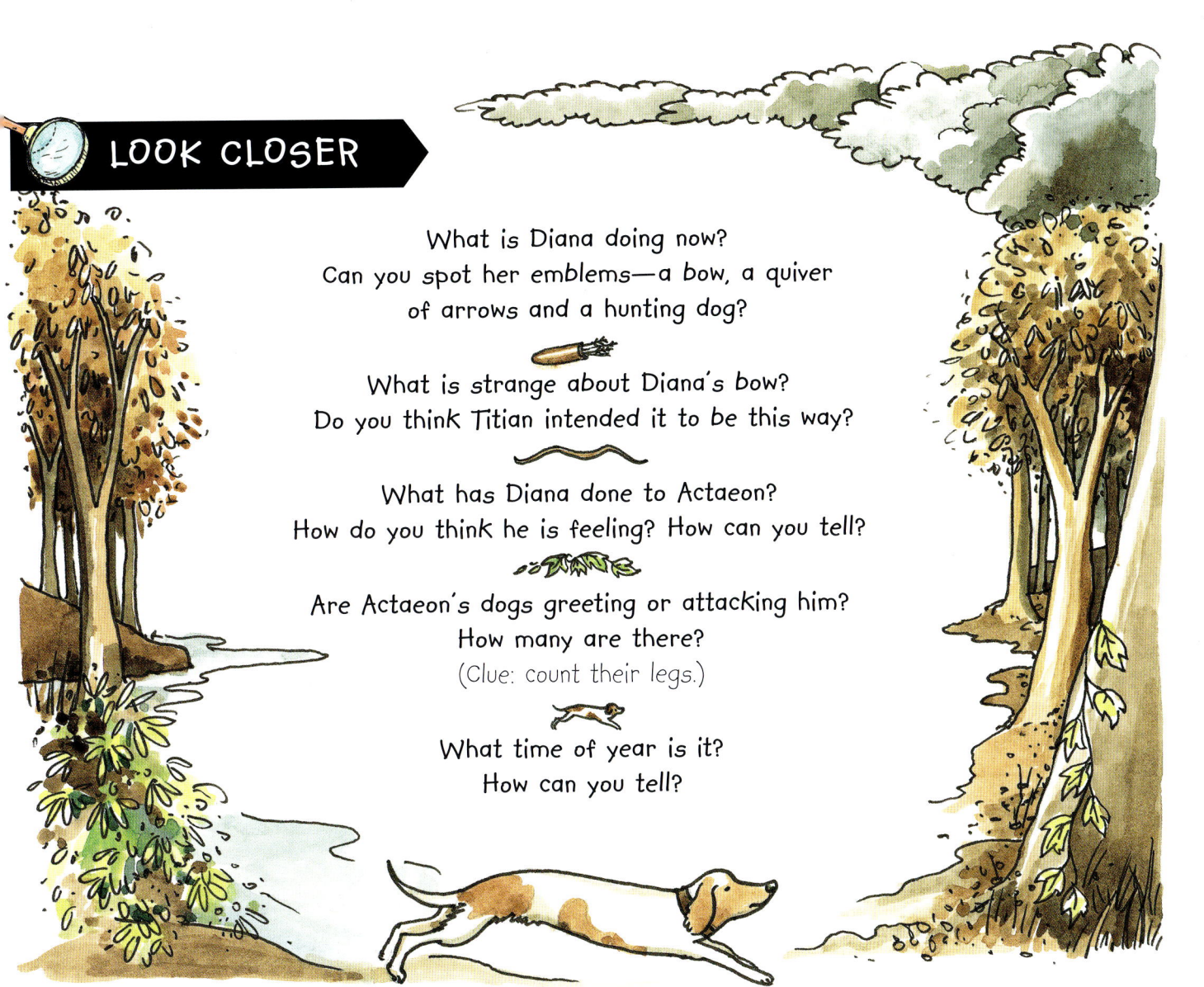

What is Diana doing now?
Can you spot her emblems—a bow, a quiver
of arrows and a hunting dog?

What is strange about Diana's bow?
Do you think Titian intended it to be this way?

What has Diana done to Actaeon?
How do you think he is feeling? How can you tell?

Are Actaeon's dogs greeting or attacking him?
How many are there?
(Clue: count their legs.)

What time of year is it?
How can you tell?

TAKE ACTION

If the picture came to life:
- what five things would be moving?
- what four sounds might you hear?
- what could you smell?

Do you think what happened
to Actaeon was fair (see page 12)?
If not, what do you think should
have happened?

Make up your own story about what happened next. Decide whether Actaeon's friend (on horseback in the background) ever discovered what happened to him.

How many different shades of
brown can you see in the picture?
Compare the colors of Actaeon
with the bush behind him.
What was Titian trying to do?

Diana and Actaeon

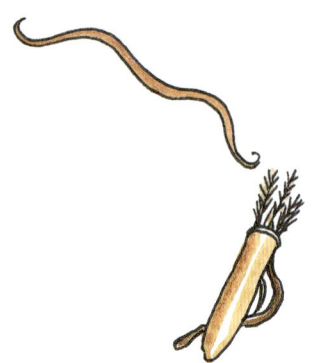

Titian, one of the most famous Italian artists ever, painted *The Death of Actaeon* for King Philip II of Spain. The picture was probably never finished and so never delivered to him. Titian based it on a myth retold by the ancient Roman poet, Ovid.

Ovid recounted how, one day, Actaeon was out hunting with a friend. While stumbling through the dense undergrowth, he came, by chance, upon Diana bathing naked in a stream. Furious at being seen, Diana laid a curse on Actaeon. He ran away, thinking he had made a lucky escape. However, on seeing his reflection in a pool, he realized that Diana had turned him into a stag.

Actaeon's own dogs, attracted by the scent of a stag, attacked him. Worse still, his friend arrived to urge on the dogs and called for Actaeon to come and watch the kill. Unable to speak, but only to grunt like a stag, Actaeon tried to escape, but his dogs bit and clawed him to death.

Titian set this story in a stormy fall landscape. Fall is the season for hunting, but also the time when plants die. See how Titian has painted Actaeon's stag head the same colors as the fading fall leaves, so that he blends in.

 **LOOK FURTHER**

A Huntsman cutting up a Dead Deer, with Two Deerhounds
(1647–60) **Jan Baptist Weenix**

Compare this gruesome hunting picture with *The Death of Actaeon*.

Which one do you think seems the more realistic?

What is the main focus of attention in this picture?

How did this hunter kill the deer?

What is happening in the background?

What similarities can you see between this picture and Titian's?

Judith in the Tent of Holofernes

(ABOUT 1622)

Johann Liss

This extremely grisly picture shows how Judith, a Jewish heroine, saved her besieged city from defeat. She and her servant tricked their way into the enemy camp where Judith cut off the head of Holofernes, the enemy general, as he slept.

 ## LOOK CLOSER

Where is Holofernes' head?
What are his eyes doing?
Where would the head be if Judith hadn't grabbed it?
What clue shows you that Holofernes was a soldier?

How would you describe the expression
on Judith's face?

How do you think her servant feels?

What tells you that Judith has only just cut
off Holofernes' head? What weapons did she use?
(Clue: look at her right hand.)

Why do you think the colors are stronger
and richer towards the bottom of the canvas?

 ## TAKE ACTION

If Judith could talk to you, what do you think she would be saying? If her servant could speak, what do you think she would tell you?

The artist painted this scene as if he were in a dark tent, shining a flashlight on the figures. **Where do you think he might be standing?**

From what you can see of Holofernes, what do you think he looked like?
- tall or short
- strong or weak
- handsome or ugly

Imagine that you are Judith, returning to your city with Holofernes' head in a sack. Describe your adventure, from beginning to end, to the friendly guard who stops you at the city gate.

 READ ABOUT

Judith, the Heroine

Thousands of years ago, the Assyrian army, led by the general Holofernes, besieged the city of Bethulia in Judah. Judith decided to save her starving city. She and her maid went to the army camp, pretending to be deserters.

After a large feast in the general's tent, Judith was left alone with Holofernes. He had drunk far too much wine with his meal and soon fell asleep. Judith snatched his heavy sword and cut off his head.

The two women returned to Bethulia, carrying Holofernes' head in a big sack to prove he was dead. Lost without their leader, the Assyrians fled. Judith and the people of Bethulia were saved.

The story of Judith comes from a collection of stories which some people think of as part of the Bible. Liss, a German painter who worked in Italy, specialized in religious stories and painted more than one version of this picture. He was very skilled at painting the human body from unusual, difficult views.

 **LOOK FURTHER**

Judith
(ABOUT 1678) Eglon Hendrick van der Neer

In this picture of Judith, it is hard to believe that such a well-dressed woman could have just committed murder.

It is probably a portrait of a woman called Judith, who wanted to be painted in the role of her heroic namesake.

How has the painter made Judith stand out?

What is she holding that hints at the gruesome murder of Holofernes?

What clues show that the woman was rich?

What is the maid doing?

What clue suggests that Holofernes was a soldier?

17

Vanitas Still Life

(1648)

Jan Jansz. Treck

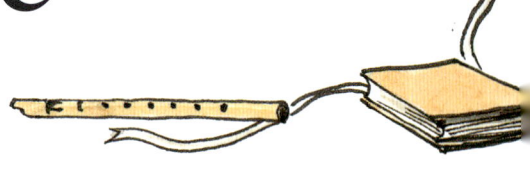

At first glance, this quiet still life might not seem very grisly to you. However, the skull is a clue that each object contains a secret message. They have all, in fact, been carefully chosen to make viewers think about death and how quickly life goes by.

LOOK CLOSER

Find something which measures time.
Find an object which has been snuffed out.

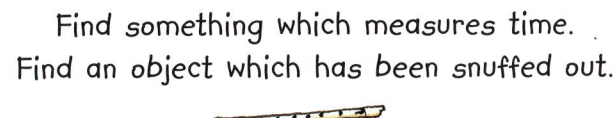

What two musical instruments can you see?
(Clue: one has a bow.)

Which three things suggest learning and knowledge?

Which two objects suggest wealth and luxury?

What do you think the straw and shell were used for?
(Clue: the shell contains soapy water.)

Which object looks closest to you?
Which one looks furthest away?

Which object looks lightest?
Which object looks darkest?

TAKE ACTION

If you could touch the objects, how would each one feel?
- soft
- hard
- smooth
- rough
- stiff
- cold

Can you find something:
- you could pour?
- you could wear?
- you could smell?
- you could keep things in?
- you could play?
- you could blow?

To paint this picture, the artist 'probably' arranged real objects on a real table.
Where do you think he stood to paint his arrangement?
- near or far away
- high or low

How has the artist arranged the objects on the table to make sure you can easily see:
- the figure in the drawing?
- the title page of the book behind the jar?
- the skull?
- the seal of the official document?

19

Vanitas Paintings

Still life paintings usually show objects—such as food and drink, dishes, and glasses—arranged on a table. "Vanitas" are a particular kind of still life, popular 400 years ago in Holland, where people were very influenced by their reading of the Bible. The word "vanitas" comes from a passage in the Latin version of the Bible, declaring that all human life is in vain if it is not lived with God in mind.

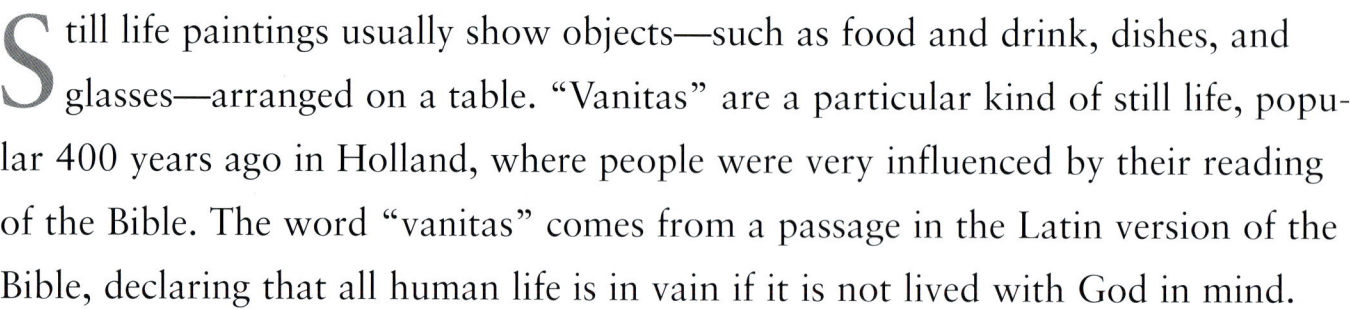

The skull is a symbol of death. The helmet is a reminder that armor cannot protect even the greatest warrior from death. The hourglass measures how time passes. The pipe and the plug of tobacco suggest that life is like smoke—here for a while, and then gone forever. The shell and straw, used for blowing bubbles, suggest that life is fragile, like a bubble. The book of music and the instruments suggest that life is like a melody—heard for a while and then silent.

The artist may have meant to make us think gloomy thoughts about life on earth. Yet his picture continues to give people pleasure almost four hundred years after it was painted. We can almost smell the tobacco and feel the silk fabric and the soft leather binding of the books.

LOOK FURTHER

Still Life: An Allegory of the Vanities of Human Life
(ABOUT 1640) **Harmen Steenwyck**

Steenwyck's *Vanitas* was painted at almost the same time as Treck's.

The two pictures have eight similarities. Can you find them all?

The shell and the Japanese sword were both rare objects at the time this picture was painted.
What do you think they suggest?

Where might the rays of light be shining from?

What measures time in this painting?

What musical instruments can you see?

21

Perseus turning Phineas and his Followers to Stone

(EARLY 1680s) **Luca Giordano**

Imagine that you have just arrived at this extraordinary wedding feast of Perseus and princess Andromeda. You find Perseus being attacked by Phineas and his men. To save himself from his attackers, Perseus is holding up the magical head of Medusa, a snake-haired monster.

LOOK CLOSER

How has the artist made Perseus and Medusa stand out?

What do you think was happening just before the moment shown here?

How does the head of Medusa help Perseus? What happens when people look into her eyes?
(Clue: look at the positions and skin color of the attackers.)

Find Phineas shielded behind two of his men. What do you think the artist is telling you about Phineas' character?

If you were Perseus, what would you have said to Andromeda and her parents, the King and the queen, just before you held up Medusa's head?
(Clue: which way are they looking?)

TAKE ACTION

Spot three things that show this picture is set at a wedding feast.

Can you find something:
- yellow?
- blue?
- white?
- shiny?
- sharp?
- gory?

Look in a mirror and make a face like Medusa's with scary, staring eyes and a gaping mouth.

Play this game with a friend. Pretend you are soldiers with spears who have been turned to stone. Stand as still as you possibly can on one leg. Who is last to move?

The artist has painted this event as if it were taking place on the stage of a theater. What two clues suggest this?

The story of Perseus and Andromeda

Perseus is the mythical Greek hero who killed a sea monster, which was about to eat Andromeda alive. On his way home from cutting off the head of Medusa, a grotesque and horrifying snake-haired Gorgon, Perseus had spotted Andromeda, a king's daughter, chained naked to a rock.

Medusa's ghastly glance immediately turned people to stone—Perseus had only been able to chop off her head by looking at her reflection in his highly polished shield. From that moment on, he kept her severed head in a bag around his waist for safety.

As a reward for killing the sea monster, Perseus asked the king for Andromeda's hand in marriage. There was a huge wedding party. The jealous and cowardly Phineas, who had previously been promised Andromeda as his bride, stormed into the party with his men, planning to kill Perseus.

Having warned Andromeda and her parents to turn away, Perseus quickly pulled out the ghastly head of Medusa. Her staring eyes immediately froze Phineas and his followers to the spot and their flesh was transformed into cool, hard, gray stone.

 **LOOK FURTHER**

Perseus and Andromeda
(1635–1700) **After Guido Reni**

This picture shows an earlier part of Perseus' story than Giordano's painting. Andromeda is chained fast to a rock, left there by her father, the king.

She is a sacrifice for the sea serpent that was troubling her country. Perseus, flying overhead, has spotted her and will soon come to her rescue.

What do you think Andromeda is doing?

How does the cloth around her help to emphasize her actions?

How would you describe Andromeda's expression?

How is Perseus traveling? (Its name is Pegasus.)

The Execution of Lady Jane Grey

(1833) **Paul Delaroche**

Think how gruesome it would be if you were asked to witness what is about to happen in this picture. It is based on a true historical event which took place hundreds of years ago.

  ## LOOK CLOSER

What is about to happen to the girl in white?

Who is the man holding the ax?
Who do you think the two sad women might be?

Do you think the girl looks innocent or guilty?
Why do you think this?

How do you think the artist felt about her
and how has he shown his feelings?

How has the artist made the picture look
as if it were set on a stage?

 ## TAKE ACTION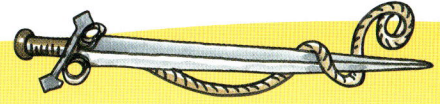

Can you find something in the picture made from each of these materials?
- wood
- leather
- velvet
- metal
- silk
- stone
- fur
- gold
- satin

The picture is huge—over 6ft 6in. high—and nearly 10ft wide.
Why did the artist decide to paint it so big? What difference would it have made if he had painted it much smaller?

How has the artist made Lady Jane stand out so clearly?

Make up your own story to fit the picture. Alternatively, you and a friend could take turns to tell the story. One of you starts, reaches an exciting moment and then lets the other person take over. Use the people and things in the picture to help you imagine what happened both before and after the execution.

The story of Lady Jane Grey

Lady Jane Grey was the innocent victim of conflicts between two religious groups in England—Protestants and Catholics. After the death of the Protestant King Edward VI in 1553, Lady Jane was made Queen by people who wanted a Protestant on the throne. Although she was royal, Jane did not really have a good claim to the throne. Edward's sister, Mary, a Catholic, had the more rightful claim. So, after only nine days of being Queen, Lady Jane was beheaded at the Tower of London.

The actual execution took place outside. Lady Jane was not blindfolded, her hair was tied back, and she did not take off her dress. The executioner used a sword, not an ax, and her attendants, not the Constable of the Tower, stood beside her.

Three hundred years later, a French artist, Delaroche, imagined Jane's execution. He invented details to make viewers feel sorry for the innocent Jane. He dressed her in a white satin petticoat, blindfolded her, and showed her groping for the block, gently helped by the Constable. The executioner looks unhappy at having to cut off Jane's head. To make the picture even sadder, Jane's two servants wail and weep, unable to watch their mistress die.

LOOK FURTHER

The Beheading of John the Baptist
(ABOUT 1869)
Pierre-Cécile Puvis de Chavannes

This painting shows another execution —this time of John the Baptist. Herod, King of Israel, had been so taken by the dancing of Salome that he offered her whatever she wished. Prompted by her mother, Herodias, she asked for John the Baptist's head on a plate. Herod granted her the wish.

Whom has the artist included in this painting? What are they doing?

Compare the light and shade in the two pictures. How do they differ?

How would you describe St. John's feelings about his execution?

Compare the backgrounds of the two pictures. How do they contribute to the mood and atmosphere?

What similarities can you find between this picture and the Execution of Lady Jane Grey?

Things to do

Each one of these six activities is related to one of the pictures in this book. Before you start, look back at the painting to help you remember all about it.

Saint Michael triumphant over the Devil with the Donor Antonio Juan

Bermejo imagined that the Devil was a monster made up of different animals. Draw your own gruesome monster. Give it the head and body of two fierce animals and the claws of a bird.

The Death of Actaeon

Imagine you have the same magical powers as Diana. Draw a person turning into an animal of your choice. Add a suitable background for the animal you have chosen.

Judith in the Tent of Holofernes

Are these statements about the picture on page 14 true or false?

1. Judith is holding a sword in her right hand.
2. Holofernes' eyes are closed.
3. Holofernes' right hand has turned gray.
4. It is a sunny day outside.
5. Judith's servant is looking at Holofernes.
6. Judith has a yellow turban around her head.

30

Vanitas Still Life

Make a list of modern items that an artist might include in a Vanitas painting today. Include: a musical instrument; something that measures time; some protective clothing; something fragile: a picture and a special container. What else might you include?

Perseus turning Phineas and his Followers to Stone

Draw your own scary picture of Medusa with glaring eyes that can turn people to stone and a head covered with hissing snakes.

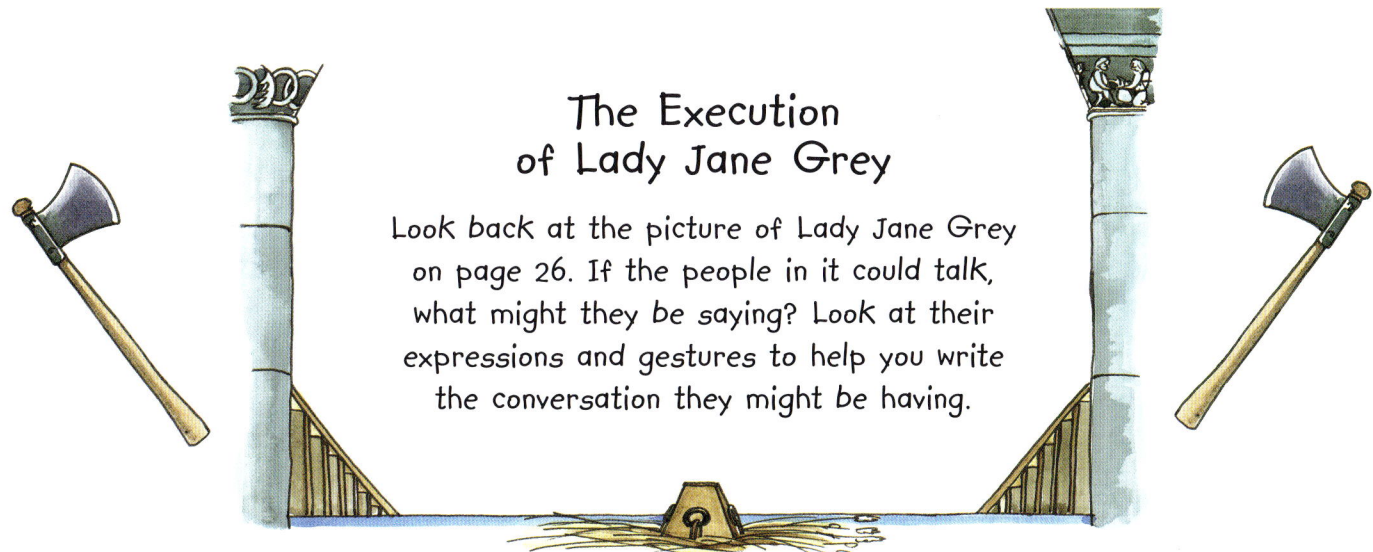

The Execution of Lady Jane Grey

Look back at the picture of Lady Jane Grey on page 26. If the people in it could talk, what might they be saying? Look at their expressions and gestures to help you write the conversation they might be having.

Glossary

altarpiece
A painting or sculpture set on or above the altar of a Christian church.

angel
A spirit, described by the Bible as an attendant of God in Heaven, and as His messenger to people on earth.

donor
A person who orders a picture from an artist, usually featuring themselves, and then gives it to a church.

emblem
Anything used like a badge to identify a person, family, or organization.

myth
A traditional story about the deeds of gods and goddesses, heroes and heroines.

parchment
A material made from animal skin on which people wrote.

still life
A painting showing mainly unmoving objects—such as fruit, flowers, or crockery.

symbol
An object painted to stand for something else. For example, a weapon may be used as a symbol of war.

Vanitas painting
A type of still-life picture with symbols of the passing of time, the shortness of life, death, and eternity. Many were painted in 17th-century Spain and Holland.

Index

altarpiece 8, 32
animals 7, 11, 12, 13, 30
Andromeda 22, 23, 24, 25
angels 6, 7, 8, 32
archangels 8
armour 8, 20

background 29, 30
Bermejo, Bartolomé 6, 7, 8, 30
 Saint Michael Triumphant over the Devil with the Donor Antonio Juan 4, 6, 7, 8, 30
Bible, the 4, 6, 16, 20

church 4, 8
colors 11, 12, 15
Crivelli, Carlo 9
 Saint Michael 9

Delaroche, Paul 26, 28
 The Execution of Lady Jane Grey 5, 26, 28, 29, 31
Devil, the 4, 6, 7, 8, 9, 30

emblem 11, 32

flowers 7

Giordano, Luca 22
 Perseus turning Phineas and his Followers to Stone 4, 22, 31
gold 7, 27

Heaven 6, 8
Holofernes 14, 15, 16, 17, 30

jewels 7
Judith 14, 15, 16, 17, 30

Lady Jane Grey 5, 26, 28, 29, 31
light 21, 29
Liss, Johann 14, 16
 Judith in the Tent of Holofernes 14, 15, 30

material 27
Medusa 22, 23, 24, 31
monster 22, 24, 30
musical instruments 19, 21, 31
myth 4, 12, 24, 32

Neer, Eglon Hendrick van der 17
 Judith 17

Pegasus 25
Perseus 4, 22, 23, 24, 25, 31
Piero della Francesca 9
 Saint Michael 9
Puvis de Chavannes, Pierre-Cécile 29
 The Beheading of John the Baptist 29

reflection 8, 12,
Reni, Guido, after 25
 Perseus and Andromeda 25

Saint Michael 4, 6, 7, 8, 9, 30
Steenwyck, Harmen 21
 Still Life: An Allegory of the Vanities of Human Life 21
still life 18, 19, 31, 32
soldier 7, 8, 15, 17, 23
symbol 20, 32

Titian 10, 11, 12
 The Death of Actaeon 10, 11, 12, 13, 30
Treck, Jan Jansz. 18
 Vanitas Still Life 18, 20, 31

Vanitas 18, 20, 31, 32

weapons 8, 15, 21, 28
Weenix, Jan Baptist 13
 A Huntsman cutting up a Dead Deer with Two Deerhounds 13